CALLIGRAPHY AND HAND LETTERING PRACTICE PAD

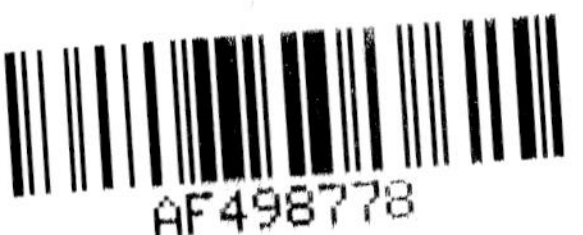

This Book Belongs to:

____

____

____

Table of Contents

Slanted angle Notepad   1-50

Alphabet practice sheets   51-100

Dot Grid Notepad   101-148

121